WATER
THE ROCKS
MAKE

WATER
THE ROCKS
MAKE

POEMS BY

David McElroy

Alaska Literary Series
University of Alaska Press
FAIRBANKS

© 2022 by University Press of Colorado

Published by University of Alaska Press
An imprint of University Press of Colorado
245 Century Circle, Suite 202
Louisville, Colorado 80027

 The University Press of Colorado is a proud member of
Association of University Presses.

The University Press of Colorado is a cooperative publishing enterprise
supported, in part, by Adams State University, Colorado State University,
Fort Lewis College, Metropolitan State University of Denver, University of
Alaska, University of Colorado, University of Northern Colorado, University
of Wyoming, Utah State University, and Western Colorado University.

∞ This paper meets the requirements of the ANSI/
NISO z39.48–1992 (Permanence of Paper).

ISBN: 978-1-60223-457-4 (paperback)
ISBN: 978-1-60223-458-1 (ebook)
https://doi.org/10.5876/9781602234581

Library of Congress Cataloging-in-Publication Data

Cataloging-in-Publication data for this title is available
online at the Library of Congress.

Cover and interior photographs © Hal Gage

IN MEMORY OF EDITH BARROWCLOUGH

Alaska Literary Series

Peggy Shumaker, Series Editor

ALASKA
LITERARY
SERIES

The Alaska Literary Series publishes poetry, fiction, and literary nonfiction. Successful manuscripts have a strong connection to Alaska or the circumpolar north, are written by people living in the far north, or both. We prefer writing that makes the northern experience available to the world, and we choose manuscripts that offer compelling literary insights into the human condition.

Contents

Land of Lost Things

What It Comes Down To

Acknowledgments

These poems have appeared in *Cirque Journal*:
Ars Poetica
At Pretrial Services
Beautiful Dangerous Women
Chemo
Elephants
House on Helluva Street
Jaundice
River Running

With gratitude for the use of the artful photographs of Hal Gage.

With appreciation for manuscript suggestions and proof reading
by Susan Ruddy shining light like a summer day.

WATER
THE ROCKS
MAKE

TURBULENCE

River Running

Here comes water the rocks make—
the chop, the chute, the tongue.
Drag an oar, slew left and tuck
into slack for the strap grabbers.

Pump rubber hard with air,
and your raft bangs through risk
and rush, wave and eddy, the suck
and heave of a stream breathing.

Sweepers comb for what floats,
meaning you, the boat, dog
barking, bottle of scotch,
bird book, and a shoe.

High snow the wind makes
holds for a moment the wolf track
over the pass, bearberry
and kinnikinnik's little bells—

for a moment the solitaire's feather.
Comes now the melt, the freeze,
the crust, corn snow, slush,
gurgle, the rivulet, and rill.

The run that runs and runs.
The whole collection, let come—
the flow, the flume, the pull
of jobs and artifacts of home,

bad love badly gone, the house,
the bones and bones, hammer
of panic, phone, car crash,
week in jail, blankets in a knot.

Let come the whole museum,
this Smithsonian you own. Let displays
the kitten makes purr and purr
in a pile, in a pool, of blue socks.

Let go the dig, the shoot, the film,
the shelved, boxed, and hung. Let it run.

House on Helluva Street

Call it right. Peter's Creek's a river
where big rocks roll and root balls gouge
banks over-hung hollow. Logjams
buck and bend the bull of the current
like bones choking a throat. Runoff melt,
glacier break, summer soaker,
some floods will take your home.

You want a clean run that lets you sleep.
After weeks of work in knee-high rapids
running gray in rock flour, with chainsaw
and chest waders, you clear the channel.
You stagger with rock after rock
in your arms deflecting current with berms
that won't let the stream eat your acres.

Woman and dog gone, you clean house.
You drop the rock in your arms.
You list your chores: get out of bed,
clean equipment, dry tents and tarps,
organize stuff for taxes, clean fridge,
organize cupboards, make the bed.
In drawers spoons full of spoons are satisfied.

They call you a shadow name
on location where you shoot.
Racing the rain, light in the lens,
spray in the boat, the story tells
of elders and seals, reflections of place
and ice, inchworm on a branch,
a clip of water poured from a boot.

Who we are and the earth around us
speak in seasons. Recycled salmon
come home to rapids in Peter's Creek
the river. The heart breaks and pumps
again. Here's your mother's stew to heat
and keep you going. I only came
to see your work and the river run.

Fishing from the Moon

The boy or girl you are rides the horn of the moon
riding low in the north where dreams dangle down,
one bare foot over Baikal, one over the Ganges.

The cockpit, the office, in your little plane is warm,
and instruments show how found or lost you are
scooting low along the coast much like the moon.

What little light there is glows tangerine,
taunting souls working down in the dark.
Reports confirm pack ice limns the world

beyond the windows. Somewhere, everywhere,
we go numb when thought and geography
float given boredom and wind enough.

But caribou and musk ox here, chiru in Tibet,
blue sheep and Marco Polo rams paw
snow and graze on what they understand.

When blizzards blow out just short of starvation,
eggs of summer bugs hatch in their lungs
and larvae feed in warm and windy rooms.

What little minds we have tunnel with voles
kenning mates and dens under tundra.
The fat distractions we call work

lumber along made large like lemmings
enhanced by routine and the daily scale,
make-work paper work mistakes we make.

How feed, how hunt for heat and home?
What logo for the story we tell? Girl jumping
off a dock, boy fishing from the moon?

In half a world of dark, half light
glows in the little globe we hoist
on our shoulders and thought stares out

like owl's eyes. A notion coming on smooth
as owl's snowy glide or quick fox pounce
presents the boy of two minds and legs

dangling down. Do you drop a line in rivers
made holy in the murk? If so, what's hooked
twisting on your question mark? Better to dive

deep lakes for the hell of it, splashing
in the cold wash at what pools around you,
talons open, wings in trail, osprey to the end?

Plain as Day

I begin to see her now plain as day
in that hot August kitchen
boiling canning jars,
her hair frizzy in the steam,
sweat running down her neck.
Oblivious to what fatigue can do,
I trot through the door
to show her a scrape
on my knee. I begin now
to see how we lived, just above
the true scrabble of poverty.
How the steer our dad butchered
and the canning our mother did
kept us alive come winter.
I had no idea what it meant
when the check
the creamery sent was five dollars.
And why would I?
We had food, we had wood
to feed the ravening beast
that made the house habitable in winter.
We had a two-holer out back
and a pump in the yard.
Mother darned my socks,
put a poultice on my knee,
and sewed my sister a prom dress.
Look at the blue velvet bodice
and white faille circle skirt
on the girl becoming strange to us
as she fills into her beauty.
See the skirt twirl out wide.
See her dance with the kitchen chair.
See the year becoming strange to us.

Mother with spare pins in her apron
and thimble on a finger,
shaking the grate awake
in the front room stove.
Mother, the mirror we come from,
leaning down with winter and fury
in her perfect hair.

Alleged Threat

I thought about going to your house and
killing you but decided it wasn't worth it.

After months of rain, divorce, mud,
artistic vision dispute, no pay,
Xanax withdrawal, and too much booze,
he cracked and sent the midnight email.

After arrest, jail, cavity search, the guard
whispering you'll love this, the hearing
from hell then bail, supervised release
24/7, ankle bracelet from hell

came months of days not knowing
the plea, trial, probation, or jail.
Winter to spring, summer to fall,
delays—prosecutor on a moose hunt.

The soundscape TV channel
writes code. Names of songs,
names of bands might mean something.
Someone listens from the fixtures,

watches from the phone, the eaves,
and cars in the cul de sac.
He digs up hundreds of small trees
from the power line right-of-way

one inch to five feet tall to plant
around his house. Buckets of loam
in the pickup—one, two, three, a pile—
from my woods to his place to feed

land the glacier left sterile. Rage,
and hurt swirl the glen, and shame
sits on the roof. On his knees he digs
and sets and tamps the seedlings in.

Call it therapy, call it Zen.
Wheelbarrow, shovel, and rake,
he's killing time, making the world
for what it's worth beautiful in ten.

Spirit of chickadee and nuthatch, spirit
of watering hose, bless him now:
come spruce, come ash,
come chokecherry hope.

All My Quarters

All my quarters look like nickels,
and the time to park is less and less.
We run to a lawyer's billable hours.
His clerk, from Uganda by way of Oxford,
walks his words with the precision
that all the time in the world allows—
the great birding back home, the best
airline to get you there, the colobus
monkeys with their white manes,
and as always the African grey,
a most intelligent bird.

We view the charges,
and do we care for some water?
His wife had to be somewhere,
so his daughter runs the office.
She sings what every four-year-old
knows from the latest Pixar.
She climbs on Dad
as we plan our plea.

She takes a deposition
from a pile spilling to the floor
and with a crayon writes her name,
something short and very red.
Probation, we learn, is all about time:
drug test, twice a week,
booze test, five per day,
the GPS ankle monitor, always,
and third-party custodian,
which is us, 24/7.

There is no safety better than Dad,
and she climbs higher, bonding,
as he explains justice.
She grabs his face, his nose,
her hands blinding his eyes.
Wobbling on his head,
she's happy up there,
and much much taller
while we are late and later,
small and smaller.

At Pretrial Services LLC

the kid with an armful of tattoos,
a do-rag on his head, and bright red boots
hyperventilates into a plastic sack.

Other young men with ankle bracelets
drink Rock Star, filling the tank,
nervous before giving a specimen.

But case worker, Big Valerie,
purple hair, glasses, fast-draw pistol
on her leg, is working the kid close.
"What's happening to me?"
And he keens like a mustang
new to hackamore and rope.

She holds his hand, gentles him
to the carpet. "Robert, look at me."
She kneels his fear to the floor.

"Slow down, I'm here, stay with me,"
big white lady with him there
on the floor where the suffering curls.

Today a moose might eat my tulips,
and somewhere lions partition a zebra colt
and for sure barrel bombs explode in Aleppo.

But here for a while, power is kind,
and the panic subsides in the young man
with the do-rag and bright red boots.

Before Trial

The defense begins with zero.
All you have is story. Rex Butler, attorney

Back to zero and rain in the boat
before your mind broke down.
Back to alder along the beach
the glacier left and the dig
for the old seal camp where the dark tools
you wade ashore film the hunt for culture.

Elaine names floes the glacier makes
where seals pup and give themselves
to hunters who prepare in special ways
for something more than luck.
With more than luck they motor
to the rocky spit where seals are cut.

George makes a loose fist and, bending
his wrist left and right, signs for bear.
The family, the house, and the bird
for which it stands take you in trust.
You see their spirit and singing place
though some songs can never be taken.

Elders name you Shadow Maker.
You shoot as old ones talk story
when nets are pulled and tides go out.
Funding promised on the come, credit debt—
they say your mind broke down.
All you have is story.

You damn the digger with a career to make,
and damn the damn government that took
the land and pays the digger to hack
for carbon and shards in muddy pits.
You learn to love the locals—overachievers some,
suicidal some, some funny, some dancing.

One by one elders take their leave and language.
Culture's lamp flares back into the earth
it came from. It speaks softly to some.
With something more than sight and sound,
we close our eyes. Owl on the hunt
glides into pearl of the evening. Listen.

When Nature Comes

Mixtec, Toltec, our own Tulum
feed into how we become.
The tribe of me and mine
scrambles stone steps to wave hello
to you and yours. From time to time
we steepen the angle of repose.

Back home the gravel we pace off
for a storage pad then rake flat
steps itself above the creek. We weave
angle iron, junk, rocks, and willow
into the edge, our redneck wattle
to slow gravity and the slough of time.

Years ago we were royalty,
or was it serfs or slaves?
Cutter in a quarry pulling rope
wet with sand along the mark,
Monte Alban builder, dreamer,
farmer, spreader of night soil?

No matter, one thought after another
rumbles on roller logs up hill,
inching into place, man hours
of pulling, greasing the skids.
Or the way Zach wires a J-box.
"Hey, it's my piano."

When Nature comes with night
and frost heaves settle the ground,
we hope this art holds the slope.
For now trees with new leaves crowd
the creek. Dressed in chartreuse,
they look foreign and a bit embarrassed.

Born to the hand working stone,
we come as the refugees we are.
We come as flesh we carry, blood,
bone, and brain. In our hopeless tongue
we claim the ground we shape
in surrender to our own nature.

Any weapons we carry are concealed
as story, light, and the mirror inside.

A Field Guide to the Birds of Peru

When we made words
they told us what we thought
they meant. Fire was fire,
cat could not be dog,
and chair was chair.
Spindles and screws,
molecules of glue,
and the polished curve
of rockers took our weight.
Thought leaned back,
crossed legs, and dreamed
a garden and life of clarity.

We made Adam walk
among the trees.
He pushed a branch aside,
and things raised their heads.
He called them elk.
Some things swam in creeks,
and he called them trout.
Some clattered into air,
and he called them grouse.
Warblers grooming the trees
kept him busy for weeks,
so hard to ID as they flit,
feed, or sing. Hummingbirds
so quick and small and green
alone took months to sort,
and flycatchers of Peru
so often high and backlit
(wing bars or not),
were hard to sight
against the light.

Winter molt, juvenile plumage,
naming was not so easy,
we said and later wrote.
Surely, the Eve we know
shook her lovely head. "Adam,
what on earth? Help me
with child care. And verbs,
don't they need more doing?"

Commentary is elementary,
of course, and there are gardens
galore where brother-to-brother
words leave much to infer.
Talk has a long way to go
to beat the great fliers. Godwits
cross the longest waters
where gyres of garbage churn.
Wheatears nesting on tundra
cross the wars of Eden
and Olduvai Gorge
to winter on savannah.
Finding ways to live
in metaphor, the wings
of words ring the wild world.

Alone in our chairs
the body of thought rises,
stepping out to learn
in one tongue or another
each jittery piece of life.
We must begin somewhere.
We raise our binoculars
close to home for scaup,

two kinds, the declensions
of sparrows, gray-cheeked,
and Swainson's thrush.
We adjust what is meant
by the feel and fall of song.
In time, the obvious birds of Peru:
condor, horned screamer,
potoo, cock of the rock,
the blue-and-gold macaw
roll into focus and begin to speak.

THE PLACE
WITHIN

Long-Tailed Boat

I am the boat you dream about.
My bow curves up, and garlands of fruit
and flowers you hang there please
the water though I pitch and plow.

Handmade under a shade tree,
I am the boat you dream about.
Practical, efficient, your reliable dream
adapted from something else.

Like glass from sand, like *Malagueña*
from cat guts strung, and plucked,
over the hole of a guitar, a Moorish kind
of boat that runs with love bitter and beautiful.

But here, logged watersheds, drought
and flood, work, and the five you love piled
on a scooter for home contribute their daily
details in our remarkable trick of happiness.

The teak pegged in my hull was once
a floor, a tree, litter in the forest soil
on hills of your childhood. My engine
has three cylinders and comes from a truck.

It tips and pivots. The long shaft and prop
can shallow over riffles, or swing
around amidships and back us
on the beach taking breakers on the bow.

Twine strung from the carburetor
to the steering shaft that is a piece of pipe
removed from a bottling factory the night
your child's fever broke is my throttle.

It threads an eye and wraps the handle.
Balancing, you stand barefoot
on the gunnels. The twist of your grip,
the push and pull of your arm gun this dream.

I am the boat you dream about.
Some nights I haul gravel upstream
running slow and deep. Some days
I zoom klongs on tours past brilliant temples

among crusts of bread for hand-fed catfish.
My upturned tapered bow all adangle with good
luck ribbons and wreathes, I rise from the mulch
of dreams like seedling teak goofy with life

and floppy leaves. Just look at me
all cobbled together, eager to serve,
your butler, your basset, your mare
rearing above the wakes of all those other boats.

Muay Thai in Chiang Mai

Boys night out, we stalk murder in the dark
or sound of it or someone sticking pigs.
My son is eighteen, and the dark we walk
is new for us. Across the car park
boom box speakers knock and knell and flute
high and low raspy squeals and flatulent blats.

Flute, bell, and drum goad good fights
and bad. The ring rises like an altar.
Cyclone fencing guards the floor
from bleacher hoi polloi. Three musicians
skirl out their atonal slaughter.
We're not bookish. My son buys the beer.

The night begins with boys and ends
with men. Each boxer climbs into the ring
and bows to the four ways. Bell and drum
beat one-two one-two for little boys
and later little men. They dance ritual
half kicks and quarter turns to each rope

and back where music is central. When it stops,
they do. The ref checks gloves and reaches deep
in the crotch for the cup and gives a good feel.
He signals; music and match begin.
They rock to rhythm, size up, feint, kick,
jab a little, their heads bobbing in time.

Action begins in the clinches with knee
strikes to thigh, side, and groin. The music,
egging on, goes double double time.
Boys fight with the ferocity of children,
but the men, like men in conference, contend
with caution and no difference of opinion.

They embrace the brotherhood of pain,
absorbing rabbit punch, gut punch,
and crotch kick, counting on the cup,
counting points leading to fatigue.
Head butt, lace-scraped eyebrow,
all honor for the badge of blood.

The critiques we impart are impartial.
This one drops his guard, fakes right,
side kicks left but no chamber,
no power. That spinning back kick
had lots of snap. That roundhouse
was sloppy. "Our Kwaja Nim Kay

would fine us push ups for that,"
my son says, who does most things
better than I. His belt is brown
while mine is red, although my arms
are strong. The night is long,
and we leave before the title match.

We cross the car park, the music
still wild but fading. We cross a bridge
arching over a river silent in the dark
returning to the woman who loves us,
not champions quite nor boxers ever
but contenders bowing before love's

daily round. We're walking in step
with silence and the dark, not brothers
quite in the music we sometimes face,
nor children to the sting of things said
and not said but adult to the stupid move
and the foot from nowhere to the head.

Panabaj

(Guatemalan village destroyed)

"My house has some water leakings,
but we're fine," writes Desiree.
"These I will fix when the rain goes.

It is correct, the river over flooded
into town, mudslides too.
Some villages vanish with the rivers."

It is fall here in the north, the month
our birds evacuate our yearly disaster.
I walk the roofline listening for geese

yelping alarm or much much nearer
the secrets nuthatch whisper to birch.
Because we face wind, fire, frost, and quake,

I fix what little I can. I check the chimney
and gutters and, since I'm looking down
at our little knoll, inspect the yard and garden.

I caulk here and there, hose out
the leaves and later, down ladder,
mulch the weaker perennials.

I recall climbing through dry corn,
at times on all fours, to the caldera's
rim then looking across the lake at Panabaj

to catch my breath. Men with bundles
of firewood on their backs using machetes
for balance came swinging down

from their daily trek hunting for fuel
while the trees climbed higher and higher
taking their leaves and their roots with them.

In Your KBRW Dream

You're droning over oval lakes
and green tundra in your plane
listening to Earl Finkler
read the weather on top
of the world with such optimism
you smile into your pillow.

"Think winter is cold here?
It's 391
below on the moon's backside."
Soon the many kinds of Eskimo snow
begin to fall, fluff, drift, stiffen,
recrystalize, desiccate, melt,

and refreeze crusty again
on the *Second Time Around Show*.
Benny Goodman tootles away,
Ella scats, and many kinds
of notes flow, blown, bent, burred,
garbled, and kissed by Satch.

Radio Reader comes back.
You're in a blizzard too bad to fly
sitting in the plane on the Tunalik
ramp, a mud box tied to each wing
to hold it down, one engine running
for radio power to lift you away.

You're sledging to the South Magnetic
Pole with Mawson. Your crewmen,
freezing, starving, demented with vitamin A
poisoning from eating sled dog liver,
turn to murder. You snug your blankets
and swim under. It's more than news.

Dream wars of the world feed
to the affiliates, and the deadening
live borough meetings go on in Inupiaq
and the awful kind of English
that paradigm shifts forward
building consensus we agree on.

Sweet dreams, the *Birthday Hour*
and *Tundra Drums* call-ins speak true.
"To Ruthie in Nuiqsut, 'Happy birthday
and many more.'" "To George at Kogru,
'It's all ok now. Coming Thursday. Meet me
at the plane and hold the dog.'"

All dreams are strange and local.
What is and was are global, but how
they mix and mean awakes in sleep.
Where time, rate, and distance solve
for here and now, the moccasin telegraph
softly walks the message home.

Rickshaws

Thirteen rickshaws line up
herringbone across the dim street
waiting for clients. The women drivers
lounge back in the paying seats
chatting, their feet in sensible shoes
propped up on the handlebars.

A passenger gets on and off they go
without a sound. A tall aerial
with colored lights illuminates
and sways like a jaunty fly rod.

Anyone looking down from a great
height in the warm, dark sky
could pick out the rickshaws
streaming through the streets
of Pitsanulok on Christmas Eve.
Small celebrations of commerce
on a human scale, they are beautiful.
Even Santa, who is a very wise man
with too many toys in his sack, would agree.

The drivers pedal us over a bridge
breathing hard over the arch
to a floating restaurant
on the Nam River.

The river swirls by in the dark.
The food is good and cheap
and paid for with soggy bills
worn from passing hand to hand.

Colored lights sparkle in the eaves.
Fireworks flare over the city,
a slight disruption of the peace
on this Christmas Eve.
You can smell the basil in your food.
You can hear the stirring
of the name in the river.

Lanquin

for Brandon

The bats came with us
and the good night fell
as we left the cave
and swam the river
back to our tent.

For a whole day wandering
in the earth
along her inner rivers,
our headlamps bobbed
bright spots along the walls
catching spray splashing
from bewildered boots.

Smoky torches
and Mayan shadows moving
on limestone
led inward to echoes
of the shaman's rattle
and prayer for the sick,
a girl kneeling
in her only clothes,
a skirt and blouse
bright and floral
in her village design,
mute with pain.
Deaf, sore neck,
eyes closed,
maybe meningitis.

Some things we think we know.
Host response: white cells
at the bottom of the bowl
of the brain,
rivers of nerves.
And what do they do?
Help little girls hear.

The crowd of white shirts
bent to work,
and we heard the bleat
and scuffle of an animal,
the kicking and grunt.

Blood smell and liquor smell
of sacrifice drove us down
passage ways
to the breath and clatter
of our own making.
Black behind us,
our spotlights spotted
sticks and stones
meant to be skull
and bones dissolving
human in the mud.

Whose work was this?
What inflammation, sore neck,
pinched nerves, anoxic,
blocked foramina,
hydrocephalus,
anatomy, and pus?

We took the only medicine
we knew.
We swam the river
as night fell
on all who hide and hurt.

The Elephants

rise pouring from the river,
easing slowly up the bank, each swaying
like a Greyhound bus pulling in.

They glide silently toward us,
graceful, tiptoeing en *pointe*,
ballerinas grown soft and thoughtful.

Tiny drivers ride their heads,
bare feet kicking behind the wings
of their ears to steer them like ships

each to a notch in the high deck
of a house. Here they are docked,
petted by the toddler Kade

and bananaed. The two points at the end
of a trunk deftly grip and twist the fruit
from his little hands and roll it up

skin and all into the pendulous lips,
heavy hanks of gray and pink
whiskery material that hides

the grinders. Country as concept
means nothing to the boy. The whole world's
exotic, something to run and touch.

Escaping his mother again,
a tall woman named Rosi
with marvelous legs, he scrambles

for a game of hide and seek
under the dripping bellies not seeing
elephants for the forest of legs.

We step aboard the rubbery backs
and wait in car seats held
front and back with logging chains.

Soon we'll move out smoothly,
silently as thought into landscape
remembered only as art,

low dikes between paddies,
arching bamboo, the white egret
unfolding and folding away.

Later, on steep trail the elephants
will have to place their four feet exactly
in tracks the size of dinner plates

or fall. These beasts once pulled logs
from the mountains ton by ton.
No more teak, they haul us

to go for a look. Do they recall their kin
in old cavalries of kings, each phalanx
trumpeting high trunks against the Khmer?

They stand so calmly deep in thought
we think while the toddler taunts his mom,
squealing from tree to tree underfoot

in the world's oldest game. Is it true
they hear the beginning heart
sloshing in Rosi's womb?

Deep beneath us the hearts we praise
big as bushels beat, but first the child
must be caught. Trunks down,

the elephants stand five square with the world.
The mountains wait in their second growth.
The camp of long neck women waits,

and the far fields of poppies blow.

In Your Running Dream

You're running from nothing, moving light
and easy, dodging left, left again, and right:
leaves and whipping branches,
dappled light, dappled shade,
others in front, more behind.
Fast footfalls are chuffing in the leaves
of red oak, white oak and bur,
buckbrush, apple and beech,
basswood and birch.
Branches lean down, dividing and dividing.
Fractals crack in the rush.
This is your fast dream.

No doubt your eyelids flutter.
You might whimper and twitch your toes
like happy dogs in the famous
Rabbit Chasing Dream 23.
Around and around in the Roman
fountain they go, splashing silver.
The sweet life glitters and the rabbit
runs seductively on forever
just out of reach and into the woods
where leaves, dead or alive, do the real work.
You're fleet of foot and never running better.

Sure, you trip sometimes, turn widdershins,
fall funny, and roll out. Your hands jam
down through this year's red
and yellow leaves, last year's brown,
and the year's before slime mold mulch
and mother dirt. The air is crisp
is all you know
and smells of fall and smoke.

What wood frogs there are
burrowed in the litter
turning their blood to sugar
becoming winter stones
are beneath your notice.

You're up again running, ducking,
dodging, choosing among pools
of gloom, shafts of light,
as room by room you frame
the architecture of place
on undulating ground,
the compounding waves of earth
gathering, pleating its fulling cloth.
You run, ducking and dodging,
the trail dividing and insinuating
among the trees. There is no happiness
quite like this, though you might fall again,
and plow your hands into rich rot, or worse,
wake.

Sukothai

Christmas is just another day
for kids in blue and white
uniforms going off to school riding
side saddle on motor scooters.
And we go off to Sukothai.

Double yellow lines mean nothing
to polite drivers smiling in the land
of smiles. No honk nor gesture
means a curse as they tear four abreast
down a two lane nearly killing you.

Supplementary reading behind us,
we put in a hard day's work climbing
terraces, shooting stupas and Buddhas
big as barns sitting serene in humid heat.
We read all the labels in the museum.

On a hill over looking the city walls
Buddha stands twelve meters tall
for a thousand years. Big as a communist
monument, he stiff arms his right hand
forward in the gesture of "no fear."

It is here we begin the hard work
of parents in reunion with our son.
Acknowledgments, tears, terms,
treaties, on each a brave new face.
Burmese legions, the coming of the Khmer,

recess. We do what families do
to feed what we can for today's hunger
and tomorrow's growth. At Wat Chang Lom
thirty-six sculpted elephants
support the large bell-shaped chedi.

Deep caked buffalo tracks pock
the once-wet field flooded by a moat
where a man and boy wade with a net.
They swirl it around, and the circumference
chain sinks the fine mesh fast from sight.
Working together they drag it up the bank,
and if there is something, no fish over an inch
and a half, they flick it in a bucket.
What once and threatened king
ever dreamed his largess would bring

the future poor such meager muddy fare?
What lost succession? What fears? What ally
must fail, fall, or drop him cold? Our son
wanders off among the ruins
and returns where we wait by the taxi

with a purring kitten cradled in his arms.
The driver nods at an encampment
of refugees by a smoky fire under a tree
hung with bitter potatoey-looking fruit
and says, "Some eat cat."

Niglik Channel Bridge

Cogito ergo sum. Descartes

If this were Rome there might be angels
on this bridge. If Paris, lovers padlocking
eternal love to rails above the famous river.
And those who think of love's weight on steel
would cut the locks preventing collapse
just in time. "I think, therefore Descartes."
With proper ID he walks head down
here on oil company tundra, thinking
about thinking. I think he likes this bridge.

If angels, if lovers lean to jig for cisco,
their lines vibrate with current alive
and brown from mountains days away.
The Colville Delta welcomes what comes
to its productive mud. Geometry
of polygon ponds and oxbow lakes
breed and hatch almost everything
that swims or flies. And watching everything,
ravens poop the pipelines white.

The Tamayayak, Sakoonung, and Niglik
flood plain channels bend and push,
sculpting noodle turns to the sea.
If you think about thinking, X and Y
grid polynomials, perhaps, or compound
such curves as Bernini carved
when stone robes in a Rome wind flap
alive on muscles of an angel's arm,
and French welders torch a lock on love.

Don't look for arches under this bridge.
Here you'll find twin steel box girders,
but time it right and a peregrine's stare drills
from a nest of sticks on angle iron.
We think Descartes and Norway's coast
taught Norwegian designers to roll this bridge
clean from one side of winter to the other.
And A to B, thought flies the Orinoco vector
to this beam in the falcon's fierce love

to beget and therefore be.

Voyage of the *Beagle*

I hate every wave in the ocean. Charles Darwin

The cabinets of England fill
with beetles from Brazil. Shells
he seemed to find everywhere
fill drawers, and prehistoric bones
are warehousing back home.

Gauchos gallop through pages
of his journal. They throw the bolas
at a cow a day to trip, kill,
and cut a chunk of haunch
to grill and eat with the hide on.

The English in him made him write.
When rivers rattle stone
it's time rolling to eternity.
"Not even the wind that blows
is so unstable as the crust of the earth."

Mud in the sea, beds where fossils
sleep in a vast museum.
What he shot or pinned in a dish
or dug from a red clay cliff
he described and copied double

for shipping home. Extinctions,
time's extension, the wasting
of the races, life breeding life
to make a better bug,
he wrote what he thought and saw.

He rode and wrote of horses
and mules, sleeping with fleas
in a hovel, what coral atolls
have to tell, the tortoise shell
variations, marine iguanas,

and famous beaks of the finches
in the Galapagos—
all building to the big idea
about which for some there
seems to be some question.

It took him years to make the case.
It took everything he survived:
the pitching of the ship spilling ink
and the ocean that from time
to time drove him to the rail.

LAND OF
LOST THINGS

Bear 747

sits in the river's Jacuzzi below the falls
waiting for the bump against his legs
that is a salmon roiling blind in bubbles.

We stare at 900 pounds of not exactly troll,
appetite of boar, the power of bear
and the falls where he stares.

A quick plunge of his head and up comes
a red flopping in his mouth. Motor-drive
cameras, each lens big as your leg, track

the head shake, water spray, and turn, his back
to the viewers, his skill at stripping skin,
meat, and eggs, feeding these tiny steps

to winter survival. Gulls gather
for scraps, and magpies peck scat
for tapeworms. "They're not human

so we give them numbers," a ranger
informs with the gravitas science inspires.
But the four-year-old sub-adult 284

splashing in the shallows, or like a hippo
snorkeling the lower river, climbing trees,
yawning, false charging through camp,

popping her jaws is something else. Raised arms
and loud talk make us big, our numbers bigger,
we think she thinks, so human we are with fate or fear,

and we call her Wild Child. The emergency call
that comes like the bear you don't see, shape shifting
in the night—thick brush, wrong number on a kill—

comes for our friend. A float pilot, who crashed
the week before and survived, arrives to fly her off
the water's wake and into the ache of air.

On bigger and bigger planes she flies
to her son who lies in a coma trussed
in the elegant machine false hope requires.

Bench pressing 350 pounds,
something happened, no name for it—
his number up—call it Freak Accident.

The bar came down and pinned his chest
causing him to regurgitate and aspirate
his breakfast, the peach that killed him.

Jaundice

Blame it on Mexico and ceviche
at the beach bar where two women
tanned and toned, in big hats
sharing stories, sit laughing
over watered down margaritas.
Blame it on hepatitis.

It's not hepatitis.
Three weeks later
a doctor in white comes,
and she's careful to say it just so,
"There is a mass."
And my wife's face crumples.

Complex procedure called Whipple.
Big cut, suction, cautery knife.
Fat white sausages of fingers grope
for hours and hours in her belly—
those big southern doctor hands.

Four or more hands in latex,
fat white sausages of fingers,
working the tangles of ducts, pancreas,
and guts in gore—so many knots to tie.

Then days of tubes, screens beeping,
numbers. But chipped ice to suck,
blankets, neck rub, foot rub, shampoo—
something about the nurse's hands
is small comfort before the agony
of seven months chemo.
Long live nurse Margarite,
the closest thing to God in ICU.

Blame it on Monsanto
for sowing farms with dragon's teeth
to poison the weeds
that sooner or later,
bit by bit, bite by bite,
poison all that lives.
Blame it on agribiz.

Blame it on fate,
the kind ancient Greeks
got so mad about,
the jealous gods harrumphing
among the boulders, cigarette butts,
and broken bottles of Olympus.

Hope and platitudes vie
against statistics
and love is not enough,
our Greek chorus chants.

Off to the side the dancers
droop their hands gracefully
finning slowly
as though treading water,
as though sleeping sharks—
who never get cancer—
are waiting for dark to feed.

Chemo

After diagnosis, Whipple Procedure,
drains put in, drains pulled out,
after they put the port in her,
they let the poison flow, poison flow.

Years from now troubadours might sit
by rivers and tune what might be lutes
to sing of bonnie nights and lady loves,
dark and light, dark and light.

Or sing how wrong we were
to half kill our lovers to fully kill
we hoped the mad mitosis
in their mad, mad cells?

Mercury, lead, and leeches
once were cures we thought,
and good wars well fought made pride
something to sing and sing about.

Like earth herself, my true love lies ill
in her cities and hamlets, and farms swarm
with drones from the medical empire
diving down her subclavian vein.

Let lutes sing and banjos plunk
of nausea, mouth sores, anemia.
Like our nation, she lies depressed by war—
damaged collateral, smart bomb errors

in a lung, a market, a wedding party,
a valve in the spleen, and a woman hoeing
in the March garden of her heart.
Bring back my bonnie, bring back her hair.

Radiation Oncology Suite

In the waiting area outside the blast doors
we leaf through magazines, waiting.
The photos suggest we buy things
to live well. On page twelve farm life
looks good, family around a bonfire,
pretty Guernsey just out of focus,
five hundred dollar handbag
attractively hung on a cedar post.

Two thoroughbreds have long eyelashes,
and the models, absurdly thin, are pouty.
And one with décolletage to the navel
suggests milk in abundance for refugee
babies. Back in the day her parents
would have smacked her bulgy ridiculous lips,
and made her clean the barn.
We don't wish any of them cancer,

but in a world out of balance, we long for
common sense, the normal and natural.
We long to go for a walk in the woods.
We stare like silent old Japanese men
in an art film. We are fierce and waiting,
backs to the large lounge windows. A cold front
massing over our shoulders, we stare
and stare, and there are so many chairs.

Supplicant

If you don't sing well, to ease her pain
rub her feet with cream from a tube,
her legs, back, and arms with lavender oil.

Each spring in the desert, villagers
old and young, angels in the clouds,
renew the adobe church with mud.

If you don't sing well, to ease her pain
give her a sip of ice water, some ice cream,
or wrap her in a soft red blanket.

Each spring in the desert, they come
on foot, horseback, and in old Fords
to rub earth and water on the church.

If you don't sing well, to ease her pain
shampoo her thinning hair. Massage
the warm foam scented with mint.

Sing or hum if you must,
comb your fingers in her hair
slowly, slowly, Pilgrim, and worship.

Grand Opening

for Dave Jackson

All his life but more so lately, his heart had a murmur.
A susurration, he might have said, a bit
of lame humor to muffle the custodian whispering
on the body's phone down in the engine room.

But there's nothing funny about back wash
through the mitral valve when the ventricle
slams its power the wrong way. Climb stairs
or hills, and you could be out of the breath of life.

We're going in, the doctors said with all the hubris
statistics on their side can bring. From the crotch
they run a snake up the femoral artery into the heart
heaving around in its bright red room.

They take a look. No question, it's a plumbing job.
They do these all the time, and time, more of it,
is what anyone wants. And in they go, unzipping
the sternum and spreading the Moorish arch

of the ribs' architecture. Machinery is called for,
stopping the heart is called for, enormous
confidence in the workings of mechanical
applications and workmanship is called for.

It all goes forth this time like a philosophical proof
whose elegance is so basic we dunderheads
nod approval. Our friend we trust will recover
this dialogue, this argument and break-in.

He will rise up with a walker and walk the hall,
will come soon to snowshoe midnights out to his bonfire,
and like the Koreans who skied across Antarctica
weak and windblown will ask for meat and whiskey.

Speakers, woofer and tweeter, in the wood box
sheltered like the heart itself will throb with ease,
music and sparks dancing up to the stars—
or overcast or heaven, if that be the case.

Trapeze

If you should leave before we thought,
I might run away with the circus and climb
above the watchers with the trapeze lady
to entertain way up there without a net.

I heard today the day of the Big Top is over.
The tents are folded and donated maybe
to refugees homeless on new continents,
but like much else we aren't quite sure this is true.

Still, we assume I will be called first,
as the saying goes, and the special caller
in the dark hoodie I try to keep an eye on
is strolling along approaching my corner.

But if you should leave before we thought,
I want to swing and fly above the crowd,
the elephants rampant, white horses trotting
with pretty ladies on their backs waving.

I want to hang like Burt Lancaster
who had a limp in the movie I saw
as a kid. I want to swing and hang
by the knees and catch the pretty lady

who is now forever you tucked in a triple spin
arching up free in a parabolic arc.
If I swing just right we catch by the wrists
convinced you are you and the air we fly through.

Mime Workshop

At the Church of Love the mimes
wear black derbies and red scarves.
They fold and crease the paper air
around a big box of nothing.

They're quiet, of course. The brush
of a sleeve along the hair of an arm
is the intake of breath a yawn makes.
An earring clicks, a shoe squeaks.

The box of air, nothing really,
goes hand to hand, mime
to mime, hand in hand
with memory of what a box is.

The Church of Love once rang
with worship by devout Koreans.
Now pomp and performance art,
silence and memory, are born again.

We believe the box, the tug of war,
and saxophone fingers running
scales in white gloves, and now
the book so elaborately read

with pages pinched and turned.
We may be dumb to the sermon
about healing and the man
lowered through the roof, but the circle

that arms make is somebody we long
to embrace, body we pray to get well,
just as we believe the pitcher,
the batter, the catcher signing heat.

If Not Answers

Mrs. Alaska plants her boot in the stirrup
of my hands, and I give her a leg up
into the cramped cargo compartment
of the small plane. Not much bigger
than the duffle bags she knees into place
on the upper shelf, she is geometry
and precision, if not poetry, in motion.

You have to admire your colleague pulling hose
in a blizzard to fuel the instrument that takes
you home. You might even admire
the wind and snow that make the world
so white and clean and safe for those
who burrow beneath the tumult, who learn
to sleep or starve and wait their way to survival.

If you wake and work under spare circumstance,
you might think to gun the engines of your limbs
and light the lights in the stadium of your brain
where games contend. What's more, this team, or that,
might invoke plays and beauty if not answers
to winning points—the warm kiss home, procedures
to save your love another year. Maybe more.

Afterthought, an extravagance to live for.

Blue Door

I am in the trailer remodel painting a door.
A laptop is drumming head-banging techno
favored by some who seem to prefer
that machinery left running on auto repeat.
I paint the door a luscious marine blue.

It has recessed panels, and I ask why.
Zach takes a drag on his e-cigarette,
bellows forth a great cloud of cold steam,
and says they can slide in grooves for expansion—
you know, humidity, hot, cold, arguments.

He can work a router, a planer, a chop saw
like nobody's business, but his girlfriend
threw him out and kept his tools. Chips fly
from the chisel he borrowed to fit the knob
in the door I painted yesterday a jealous forest green.

Taylor, no car but a beautiful teacher girlfriend
who belly dances on the side, says panels
like these came from the Middle Ages.
The divider at the top half is a cross,
and the bottom panels symbolize an open Bible.

I dip my brush into the can and slurp
a soulful blue into the recesses
of Deuteronomy, perhaps, or Psalms
whose page in the valley of the shadow
swells when someone boils cabbage.

Behind other doors maybe some
play Paul Robeson's "Deep River,"
or Sarah Vaughn glides into "Day by Day"—
the human voice that opens longing
for redemption and a fair shot at love.

Some wait for improved blood work
to allow treatments to save them,
and some watch cop shows
where pretty lady detectives
are the best shots, and some just wait.

The yin and yang of doors,
complete with brushed nickel knobs,
swing into evening and the mountains
standing by. Spiritual, practical,
warm on the inside, cold on the outside.

Opened with a key and a kiss,
or closed with a curse and a slam,
some days work us over. If shut
and primed in streaky shades of gray,
go with the truest blue you have.

No Trout

It was hard getting by. No trout. No fur.
We gardened and farmed, sold milk
to the local creamery's low prices,
sold apples out the back of our car.

Just a dreamy boy, what did I know?
I would be a trapper of mink and beaver
with flannel shirt and birch bark canoe.
I was Robin Hood with cudgel and bow.

The last elk killed in Wisconsin
hadn't bugled in a hundred years.
Every wilderness was a fenced
quarter of a quarter section.

Cleaning the barn, shoveling manure,
filling the wheelbarrow, pushing
it up the plank to the Mayan pyramid
growing in the barnyard was not adventure,

was impediment to climbing trees
or swimming naked in Freisinger's creek.
We walked a mile and a half to school,
as they say, up hill both ways.

But 4-H club led me to take a heifer
to the county fair. I washed her tail,
curried her rich brown coat, and Big
Barbara said, "Feel inside my sweater."

One night a security guard on a horse
galloped down the crowded fairway
whipping a drunk with the ends of the reins,
the man bleeding, also the horse.

I rode the Hammer, I rode the Tilt-a-Whirl.
Dizzy and rich as I'd ever be—bright lights,
my calf, music from the Merry-Go-Round,
that second soft warm firm breast in the world.

Inge's Spring

Leaf out, gardeners on the move.
Her fondest memories of the war
are soft nights after the bombs
(always in waves of three)
under the linden trees in bloom.

There are friends to check on,
bandages to roll, and food to find
while Duke and Ella swing
on BBC. There are steps to learn
under the linden trees in bloom.

Volume turned down,
"lady be good, be good to me,"
leaks into the street when gardeners
are on the move. Leaf out, blackout
under the linden trees in bloom.

You Go to Hell

and, damn it all, foes, fiends, and faint friends
from the oil business barge in spilling your glass
of ice water. No redemption, they press
through doorways; some, the smokers, speaking French.
It's all bad: diarrhea, boils, bad hair, misinformed
guards, bad lighting, leafless trees, sick robins.
If you can't rule the rock and roll in heaven
better to reign here. Grab a bullhorn
and organize chaos. For killers, the famous fire.
Pedophiles, bend over. Suck pus from wounds
of proud corpses, you politicians—proud, you said.
And nature poets, ignorant of science, inspire
your vowels to feed at latrines. Devil's dead.
Make your moony rhymes click and lick your spoons.

Burglary

Steps unshoveled, owners off somewhere
fighting cancer as best they can,
the face of the house is vacant as smiles
on a gate agent. A screwdriver rides up
in a pocket and pries open a window
with all the innocence of a common tool.

The boots that leave a smudged track
in the snow do their job to warm the feet
as they lift over the sill and violate the desk,
dropping dirt and a clot of snow
that soon must melt on a sheaf of bills
waiting for end of the month payment.

It's gloomy enough to stumble on toys
and get a nasty head bump on the cat's
climbing pole. All the jewelry of all
the women in a sleeping world
hides in ornate boxes on dressers
or in a coin purse living in a sock drawer.

No one looks for diamonds in a jar
of screws or jewels in a box of books.
Here bare fingers press gullible prints
the cops never seem to find on drawers,
and cloisonné case where pearl studs
lay their eggs, where a string of pearls

famous for its foxtrot namesake
glowed on a grandmother's throat in '41.
Earrings, necklace, bracelet,
tumble into the screwdriver pocket
wadded into a pair of panties—beige
for the mature calming warmth

they bring to a special night out
of jitters, crime, and maybe drugs.
Downstairs again, a last minute armload
of lens and cameras, rests like firewood
in the crook of a hard working elbow.
Now out to the cul-de-sac past the neighbors'

plastic inflated holiday decorations.
Kept erect and alive by an air hose,
they're a lighted confused community
of Santa, baby in a bassinet, girl,
old man, and camels who watch a wise man
bending to advise a snowman.

Looking toward the street, Spiderman
clings to an Eiffel tower. At dawn, the fan
times out and shuts off all breath. And then
they'll deflate like crowds at mass shootings—
head, trunk, and limbs—the colorful sprawl
on dance floors, in church, store, or schoolyard.

Into the maw of omnivorous night,
something that belongs to somebody,
borne from a room of someone's days
and dreams, goes not knowing how much
of theirs it is, into the great bear digesting
all that comes running and passes through.

Land of Lost Things

Three women rise from the waves
with their beauty shimmering
down their bodies as the ocean
closes where they have been.
Perhaps, the thinking goes
among the men who come later
with metal detectors sweeping
the sand, the women will shake water
from their hands like waterfowl
in the weeks before migration,
and it's then the engagement
and wedding rings fly from fingers
shrunken and pruny to the sand
where in the land of lost things
they hide for a time or forever
with odd socks, wallets,
sunglasses, keys to the van,
each unmated from its purpose,
itself entire, value unmeasured,
somewhere free in golden sand.

WHAT IT
COMES
DOWN
TO

Leaf Out

is begun, King James tells himself.
Verily, the sap is risen.
He strolls his boreal keep
to the circumpolar forest,
some of it his. He thinks of Easter,
which comes late this year,
and that business of the angel
with the big round stone.
If it takes a squadron of scribes,
he needs to make the mystery clear.

Now birds are making melody,
he recites, and in the long twilight
some are sleeping with open eye.
Day or night, ruffed grouse strut on a log.
Comes now the blessed birch,
those floral chartreuse leaves
pressing out the very engines of life.
The work in wood is begun. That,
and one yard chore after another
beats its drum, sings its native song.

Spring

The lemon-lime green of spring is upon us.
Leaf out fills winter's scattered vacancies
among the tiered dark greens of spruce.
The Pacific loons are in the news again,
and the loon cam shows nest building
on Connor Lake, and Argentina gave
back our tree swallows just in time.

With binoculars I watch a gray-cheeked thrush
open its beak. The small brown body
vibrates with effort, but all I hear
is hiss, my tinnitus. Powerful robins
come through loud and clear, but gone
are the red polls, kinglets, warblers,
and delicate love song of the chickadee.

Though ears are nearly blind with white noise,
the flimsy jury-rigged Edsel rattle-trap of love—
hot pink body, florescent chartreuse fenders—shimmies
down your streets of Havana cobble, and still
I hear you. With creative genius born from years
in our special period, no aid from nations,
oxen plowing the fields, growing our own—

my laughing loon, busy kinglet,
my little brown thrush, lover on the Malecon,
prepare to straddle my lap. With North Korean
five cylinder diesel, DeSoto transmission,
Toyota brakes, clothes hanger aerial, wipers
by Lada, red streamers on my fins—
behold, I come.

Spring Snow

A foot of snow, more falling, day closing in,
and the husband stuff I'm saying,
"work can wait, don't go," doesn't take.
So I drive my wife out to the main road
and walk home in drifting memory.

A neighbor, Debbie the dentist, divorced,
backs out, smiles hello, and spins off to peer
into the volcano of someone's cavity. Lola,
her three-legged black Lab, whines from deep
in her pen along with Toby, the randiest springer

to ever hump my leg. I used to know
the names of all the dogs on our road,
but now I don't get out much unless weather
or downed trees opens us up to brag
about disaster, and we pet each other's pets.

The snow so muffles noise that a white car
comes breathing by with a driver
I don't know. But I do know Saysha
next door, a something-special breed
for three boys allergic to other dogs.

She used to be fast, and Jonas called and called
and chased her all over the neighborhood.
When Wade was five, Tyrannosaurus roamed
our woods. You had to be on the lookout.
He's six-eight and a doctor soon.

Torry, the middle one, found himself
lost between earphones of sacred music,
and judging by the face where thoughts
collide, it's composed of guitars,
smoky women, garlic, and stolen fire.

In the house on steroids across the road
there lived a little boy and an ugly pug,
and Ruby was her name. She threw a fit
each time we passed, and the boy would scream
like Stanley in *A Streetcar Named Desire*,

"Ruby, Ruby, come back, Ruby."
And they all come back: Katy, Kobuk, Isaac, Ibeck,
and Rose, Stormy the sheepdog, Butch and Ben,
gorgeous stupid huskies, dead from porcupine
quills and shotgun pellets in a pullet house.

And Terrapin, the Gordon setter, who lived off the grid
with Mark and Carol up the hill. When storms
plugged the road with deep packed snow
or froze their spring or blew out a window,
we helped with shovels, jerrican, or plywood.

Each year Mark baked the first king. We'd circle
to watch that king on coals in snow with Joplin
and The Dead squalling from speakers gust by gust.
Mark was the last I knew to cut his ponytail.
Terrapin made it to 17, fastest dog I ever saw,

but eventually the grace and power left him
to reside elsewhere, perhaps in that heeler
three doors down leaping in a window
barking at the intruder I seem to be—
man trudging with a ragged pack of ghosts

intent on picking the locked doors of thought.
It will take frontal passage, a power nap,
and hour of shoveling tons of this boreal beauty
to clear the steps and drive. For now the spruce
lower their arms, and young birch supple as girls

bow down as lace and satin from heaven
descend slowly like Stella curving downstairs
to her baying brute. Misfortune squats
no doubt in that house and for sure this one—
Big Rex in the room—and we keep a lookout

for each twinge and the bills he brings,
but who remembers rigid children on porches
freezing in last year's news? We rely on the kindness
of time and forgetting—solstice, lilacs and long light,
windows open, doors open, arms out wide.

Dancer in the Rain

Shovel to shovel we dig.
Each step, the blades knife
into wet, black dirt
where the raspberries grow.

Dancer with a green thumb,
leaving a house and life,
she wants what's green
to follow to new gardens.

Pas de deux, what a pair
we are: my son's friend—
or something more than friend—
and I in shaggy winter coat.

In cargo pants and boots,
our Giselle, vernal beauty,
bows to her work digging
as rain drips from her chin.

In my shaggy coat no one sees
how I lift and pivot
as bushes we bring turn
and step into my empty rows.

Anchorage Opera Shop

The story of love is best told with props.
A blushing divorcée and her simple swain
kiss over wild wilted roses in his hand.
Autumn love can always use a dog—
German shepherd loyal to a fault,
or golden retriever, scatter-brained
but affable as love in your sixties
or even after as is too often shown.

If your father is a clown, your spouse
a jealous Moor, or the chief of police
wants in your pants, you know
that a scarf, lost letter, some kind of mask
or lie will move or muddy the plot.
If your TB is acting up and the flat is cold,
you cough, somehow sing, but rest assured
someone is burning their poems for heat.

To make a production of your love,
you need a back story back stage.
You need a shop. You need lumber
to set you up, shelving with tangles
of electrical cords and cans of lights,
spots and floods to highlight hope
and color wheels to stain betrayal,
a sound board to hum your heart.

You need Roman breast plates,
open cans of dried paint, thrones,
ladders, chariots, and a butter churn.
You need racks of complicated clothes
with tassels, bustles, and ruffs. You need
binder twine. You need a barrel of brooms
to sweep away scraps and sawdust
from the last show when Tosca jumped.

You might live your life for art,
be a jester with a Styrofoam hump,
or work at the cigarette factory.
You might need this rubber knife,
might need this parapet on tiny wheels,
and the foam mattress to fall into,
or this fly rod to fly again your rebellious
oiseau, the stuffed bird of love.

All the Things about Horses

All the things about horses hard to explain
are telling us what they mean.
Clydesdales churning through powder snow,
the Arab's ankles flexing, arch of the neck,
lift of tail, delicate muzzle drinking tea in a cup,
and the great Percheron bearing the girl
and her armor into battle, lather flecking
his dappled gray coat, and the inner voices
she hears that he hears
come speaking to us now.

When the moon was half a man,
when earth was new, when water thickened,
and the great sorrel balls of mud
rolled on their backs, feet in the air,
curving their necks, nostrils flaring,
the old fear of the great cats
deep within their eyes so quick to startle
from paper scraps or butterflies
yet patient in harness and rain,
they came lurching up
from the valley in which they were made,
and the rich round rumps drove them out.

When the light they move in
is warming the wind and pinking the clouds,
and the soul takes off goodness knows where,
the paints and bays are trotting out
floating over rolling hills of soil and swale,
their manes lifting and lifting.
Where the prairie chickens drum
and prairie dogs whistle,
they come and come.

Where before ends and after begins.
Where when you go down,
you gray into sage,
you green into grass.

I wear floppy things. I lie down.

for Merrily Weisbord

The hand knows a peach when it sees one.
The tongue knows a name when it hears one.
Tree on the mountain,
white goats in the slide rock,
lips of the wind whispering a little something
from the love queen of Malabar.

The burn barrel crackles, is prayer
flaring in mist. Fire that is spirit
is music played and played.
Ice free, the river pours new
and new over old round rocks—
"the hungry haste of rivers in me."

The physics of making meaning,
how can that rush be shown?
The far scene, the close crocus?
What touch or tale to tell
the fuzz of, the juice of,
the quantum of want coming real?

I reach for a V of geese that cackles
overhead. Feeling its way, the hand
holds a cloud, sees a tree on the mountain,
white goats in the slide rock,
knows the smell in spring of leaf litter I lie on
where leaves and loam make my cradle.

Beautiful Dangerous Women

In the movies, Eva Marie Saint rode the train
north by northwest. In life forty years later,
that tight-sweatered double entendre temptress
flew just north with her very nice husband
where in a buffet line reaching for broccoli
I accidentally bumped her elbow.
I smiled my "excuse me" and she smiled hers.
Beautiful as ever, just what did she mean by that?
Too soon, my Cary Grant moment dissolved
in gravy spilled in dollops on salad.

Me attracting beautiful women? Why else
would Sharon Stone fixate on a Talavera
platter handled moments before by me?
I remember it so clearly: Old Mexico,
Guaymas, the sea, tourist trap,
over-loaded shelving. She in cutoffs,
I'm sure it was she, and T-shirt,
no makeup, a stunner no matter what,
but looking real. She set the plate
back down, but I could see we shared a
similar taste for hand work of artisans,
active patterns, bright colors,
and the meretricious glamour of surface
glaze. She left, and I, plain and simple man,
watched her leave and bought that plate.

What It Comes Down To

What it comes down to is a warm bed,
food, someone to love who loves you—
in short, Maslow's hierarchy of needs,
and for some a good dog and a good cat.

When Chula and Shere Khan foam
around my legs they want to be fed
and over fed. They wag and whine.
They flirt their gorgeous eyes at me,

the food junkies, and I, pusherman,
love them and their fur for it.
They stir my a-bit-to-the-left
self-centered heart. I scratch their ears,

pet, and pander, give them succor.
They activate my beneficence gene
to slake their wants and needs with kibble.
Saint Francis would be proud—but humble.

In the story he walked from Assisi
to Gubbio, a charming town worth a visit
if you are not pressed for time,
and told a wolf to stop eating people

because we are all made in God's image—
meaning shop keeper needing teeth,
kids with solemn toes and runny noses,
the Jew, and the Moor's wife who has jaundice.

Of course there were maidens fair
to cook, change babies, bathe the elderly.
Swains there were as well to woo and build
a church, still there, with prayers and swearing,

sweat and stone. Saint and wolf
shook hand and paw, and neither killed
anything after that. Peace ruled;
saint ate bread and wolf ate clover.

In other news new wolves hunt
Yellowstone and the ranchers are angry.
What would Francis do? Beauty queens
call for peace above their cleavage.

Peace everywhere—along Montana's
ranges, the elegant arches of Aleppo,
windswept plains of the dinner table,
and down in the gullies of our groins.

O night, winter night, let come
warm beds where lion and lamb,
good dog, good cat, lie down together.
Let educated angels descend

to make atmospherics of physics
quickly flock the forest of spruce
with snow. Slower seraphim going tree
to tree with magic wands would take weeks—

but what is time to an angel?
Thinking small as mankind does,
what works the most day in day out
is the way we look, the tribe we are.

We string lights, shovel steps,
and tighten front door hinge screws.
Unstuck, we pretend it opens easy for all.
Come right in, we say, don't mind the dog.

Musical Instrument Museum

A pair of cactus wrens is having lunch
outside the window, pecking the ground
where nutrients hide, as we sit inside
on tall chairs eating turkey on rye.

Later we wander the US section,
saving the rest of the world for later
as we do in life while Yupik and Yaqui
dancers drum and chant live in video.

Mankind will make music
from anything with a skin, a string,
a tube, a hole, a pick, a stick,
but here is a preponderance of guitars.
The story of Martin, the story of Fender.

From Beale Street to Motown,
Grand Ol' Opry to Joplin, Hendrix
to Hancock, opera to gospel—
in black and white they sweat
the same, and soul sings in reeds

and strings. The gizmos of piano wood
and wire sing, and so does the story of luthiers,
their jigs and glue, each voluptuous box
where sound, where sound, resolves.

Long brass tubes bend and bend
with valves. The polish on the curve
and swell of the saxophone bell glitters
gold in the '50s at the Blue Note.

And here is Coltrane sucking in darkness
from a smoky room. He fiddles with air
and blows out "Equinox" slow and cool,
for a moment his soul on loan to the night.

The notes shimmer and glow for us
like leaves in slow wind that shiver
and turn the light on all creeping things.

Ars Poetica

Never begin with a bucket of shims.

Open with red stilettoes
cupping the lovely feet
of flight attendants tick-tocking
the black glass floor
through Barcelona International.
Welcome impalas pulling roller bags,
breaking everyone's train of thought.

All trades, the gear tackle and trim,
the varied carols.

If you quote, quote your betters.
If you plant, plant your beauties close.
Not much art, not much weed.
Go for abundance, go for broke.

Time on flowers is good time.
Peonies done, delphiniums mostly,
bee balm coming on strong and red
along with lilies, mostly yellow, some orange
and spotted tiger lilies, too.
If your winters are long and summers cool,
Himalayan poppies, frilly and blue,
stand tall for something beyond words
and sing verse after verse the gospel
of mulch and protozoans,
their own hosannas,
Jesu, joy of man's desiring,
beneath the watching trees.

Power wash the deck, hose out
your gutters, rotate your tires.
Dog down your lugs.
Shoulder in and torque to blue torque.
Calm your winter bear,
and rejoice in traction,
time in snow light,
time in the dark.

If you explain thunder to your dog
quivering between your legs,
you can mention Sarajevo and Selma,
pick one, and, though it's been done, Troy.
Vukovar is good if you have been there,
and Wounded Knee is always here.

If you explain your lover's beauty,
mention hunting and gathering,
oatmeal and agriculture,
bones inside the kiss,
and the cuneiform bones writing
the curious poems of the feet.

Admire the time you stop
at red lights. Your lover's disease
and the woman crossing the street
remind you of cut-away charts
in the doctor's office. Muscles,
arteries, and veins rivering up and down
inside her skin, and the heart working overtime
like Kenny the plow guy in big snow.
The bones, the guts, small and big

snaking north to south, the great purple lake
of the unsung liver, the pancreas
lying like a sea cucumber
against the spine under the stomach
seeping juices to keep her alive.
You see her shiny hair
bouncing with each step,
and see the bravery of bones
shimming the intricate feet
in leather boots tick-tocking concrete.
You see the tiny spot growing on her lung.

If you read from your work,
go to your nearest garage.
Lift high the lube rack.
Let hydraulics expose the belly
of your Mazda, her sway bar,
oil pan, differential, and tranny,
all the muddy, knuckly stuff
of transport. Seat lovers
of the spoken word on stacks
of tires and pickup beds,
anything handy, a bucket of shims.

Marathon Battery calendar pinups
line memory's walls. Air hoses coil,
and fan belts loop above the bench
where mind and heart assemble the bolts,
bushings, and blood, the sticky note
metaphors, the O-rings oohing and aahing,
the washers and gaskets, last year's bird's nest,
and an earring. Sign your books on the hood

of someone's beloved Studebaker
centered in the richness of messy work.

Go to a hospital or butcher shop
where hanks of haunch drip from hooks.
Carefully note the chopping blocks
set with hors d'oeuvres,
code blue up in 5-0-2,
pink tassels twirling overhead
on ceiling fans, books CAT-scanned,
pulse taken, dumped on scales
and sold by the pound, celebration
of place where things that matter happen.

Visit your landfill where matter that happened
rots in midden. Where rats and rot
change the past to other things—
Argentine mothers marching the plaza
to shame the world and bring other things—
husbands returned, sons and daughters
made whole, Vukovar festive, Kirkuk diverse,
bison calving, Lakotas grilling hump
in the back yard, cracking fat from marrow bones,
and woman, woman dancing in a jingle dress.

Where plastic diapers deliquesce to peat
in five hundred years, we hope, dig deep
to mine a dream of the winter bear.
With paddle ears and doofus nose,
with intricate lips feeding
on shadows twig by twig, build
the yearling moose you think you know

line by line ungainly as the train of thought
that walks you here.

Roll back the busted toilets of time.
Find and fold velvet seat covers to stitch
the floppy antlers of June.
Bend the long legs over blowdowns,
and stand them tall to blend with roadside alders.

What you write means nothing for most,
an ear flicker shadow in shadow,
good for nothing, a rustle in the brush,
honey gone from a plastic squeeze bear.
Still, in silence, as any beast will tell you,
there is domain in vast holdings
beyond saying in weeds or words.

Let spring stir and study the dump.
Let grass in wind flow like water
to heal our souls and soil.
Defending us, the trees leaf out in battle,
and the long tongue of the cub bear
licks the wish and history
congealed in your empty bottle.